BRITISH POSTCARDS
OF THE
FIRST WORLD WAR

Peter Doyle

YOU NEVER KNOW WHAT YOU CAN DO 'TILL YOU TRY.

SHIRE PUBLICATIONS

Published in Great Britain in 2010 by Shire Publications
Ltd, Midland House, West Way, Botley, Oxford OX2 0PH,
United Kingdom.
44-02 23rd Street, Suite 219, Long Island City, NY 11101,
USA

E-mail: shire@shirebooks.co.uk   www.shirebooks.co.uk

© 2010 Peter Doyle.

A CIP catalogue record for this book is available from the
British Library.

Shire Library no. 582   •   ISBN-13: 978 0 74780 766 7

Peter Doyle has asserted his right under the Copyright,
Designs and Patents Act, 1988, to be identified as the
author of this book.

Designed by Tony Truscott Designs, West Sussex, UK
and typeset in Perpetua and Gill Sans.
Printed in China through Worldprint Ltd.

10 11 12 13 14   10 9 8 7 6 5 4 3 2 1

COVER IMAGE
A selection of British postcards from the First World War.

TITLE PAGE IMAGE
Artist Dudley Buxton's illustration 'Tommy' and 'Jack' –
the mainstay of the British armed forces. Card published
by Beagles and Co., of London.

CONTENTS PAGE IMAGE
Typical cards from the period: patriotic, humorous, even
sentimental. Field Marshal Sir John French (centre) was
Commander-in-Chief in 1914–15.

ACKNOWLEDGEMENTS
I am grateful to the postcard publishers for the rich legacy
they have left for the historian. I would like to thank Bella
Bennett, Steve Henderson and Steve Wheeler for sourcing
some interesting cards; all others are from my collection.
Julie and James, as ever, are my constant inspiration.

Shire Publications is supporting the Woodland Trust, the UK's leading woodland conservation charity, by funding the dedication of trees.

CONTENTS

THE PICTURE POSTCARD GOES TO WAR

Fascinating to collectors and social historians alike, postcards of the First World War illustrate many forgotten aspects of the conflict, their images loaded with meaning, their written messages providing insights into the developing machinery of modern warfare. The purpose of this book is to provide a guide to the main themes covered by these contemporary cards.

A study of the postcards of the Great War period provides a microcosm of the war itself, a representation in pictures of the combatants, the nature of war and the feelings of the British people at a signal moment in their history. During the years 1914–18, at the height of its 'Golden Age', the postcard was ubiquitous: worldwide in use and popularity. Postcards were sent (and collected avidly) by civilian and soldier alike, and were to cross all social boundaries, from the lowliest private soldier to the loftiest general officer. British postcards of the period differ substantially from those produced by their friends and enemies alike. Less sentimental (though sentimentality is a feature of early war cards), perhaps more understated and gently humorous, tracking the development of the postcard through the war years provides a unique insight into the response of the British people to the horrors of the war.

THE POSTCARD

The postcard had humble beginnings. Born in the Austro-Hungarian Empire in 1869, postcards were at first unglamorous, intent on providing a convenient means of sending short messages through the postal service. Plain and unpretentious, there was no need for separate envelopes and writing paper, sealing wax or any of the other paraphernalia that typified Victorian correspondence. Quick to use and effective at distributing brief messages, the experiment was to spread rapidly across Europe. The simplicity of the concept ensured its success.

Reaching Britain in 1870, the postcard was subject to scrutiny from the Post Office, whose rules had to be continually adjusted throughout the latter part of the nineteenth century to accommodate them. Critical to the success

Opposite:
'Flag postcards'
from various
publishers,
highlighting the
flags of the Allies
(see pages 8–9).

5

of the experiment was the possibility of posting at half the normal letter rate – a halfpenny. Subject to stringent Post Office regulations, to qualify for this rate the postcard was to be composed of a simple card with two essentially blank sides – one for the address, the other for the message, emphasising the functionality of its purpose. Postage was already paid; the card had the halfpenny stamp printed upon it by the Post Office, hampering private enterprise. And, as address and message were not to be mixed on the same side (a stipulation that carried with it the penalty of full postage rate if ignored), there was little possibility of any other devices or illustrations being carried on the card.

This bureaucratic battleground meant that the picture postcard took some time to take off in Britain, while from mainland Europe came alluring continental views of mountains and waterfalls, lithographed and in colour, produced at the cutting edge of the reproduction technology of the time. Critical to the success of the postcard was discussion in Parliament of the

Early picture postcards from 1902. With an undivided back, space was limited for the message, in this case written on the same side as the illustration. Published by Raphael Tuck & Sons.

weighty matter of whether an adhesive stamp could be affixed to a card, thereby permitting other manufacturers other than the Post Office to create them. The break-through came in 1897 when card backs were divided into two halves – one for the address (on the right), one for the message (left) – with a space top right for the adherence of the stamp. This left the front free for an illustration, and with official approval for stamps finally to be stuck to cards, came the birth of what collectors call 'The Golden Age' of postcards. From 1902 (the delay caused perhaps by the shock of the Post Office sweeping away its former objections) to the introduction of the one-penny rate in 1918, the picture postcard was a runaway success.

During their 'Golden Age', postcards achieved multi-functionality. They were now sent to recipients with the express purpose of 'adding to their collection', or were bought simply as souvenirs and collected in lavishly produced albums. But they were just as easily ephemeral, used simply to pass on mundane messages about tea engagements and other brief liaisons. The Golden Age of postcards also happens to correspond to the period of sustained warfare that commenced with the largest of Britain's Victorian wars, the Second Boer War of 1899–1902, and which ended with the much larger conflict of 1914–18. During the Boer War, many publishers (particularly Raphael Tuck & Sons) made their names – and the reputations of artists such as R. Caton Woodville and Harry Payne – from the depiction of soldiers in colourful uniforms, somewhat different from the actuality of the warfare as prosecuted on the dusty veldt of South Africa.

Patriotic cards in this manner were also to announce the arrival of the First World War, when the European nations went to war following the tensions that erupted in the Balkans in 1914. With war declared by Austria-Hungary with Serbia on 28 July, the major powers followed in committing to what was to become five years of slaughter; by the Armistice of 11 November 1918, the death toll from a conflict fought on three continents was to reach ten million military deaths, twice that many in total. One in six British families would suffer bereavement.

Postcard commemorating the declaration of war in 1914. Sent to America, it is unusual in having a sprig of heather attached, for luck.

BRITAIN DECLARED WAR AGAINST GERMANY
Wednesday, August 5, 1914.

"God Save the King."

Oh, the
bonnie,
bonnie Heather.
Let it bring
to you my friend all
the Gladness
and the Sunshine, and the
Joy that has no end.

A Sprig o'
Hielan' Heather.

7

ALLIES

The 'postcard war' opened with a wave of patriotism. In the summer of 1914 the march to war was rapid. The assassination by Serbian activists of the heir to the Hapsburg Empire, Archduke Franz Ferdinand and his wife Sophie, on the streets of Sarajevo on 28 June is well known as the spark that set Europe alight. The ultimatum to Serbia that followed was to provide the kindling; it was not long before the whole of Europe was ablaze, a consequence of alliances, understandings and secret military plans.

For Britain, it was the loose *Entente Cordiale* with France in 1904 – and another with Russia in 1907 (together with the alliance of France with Russia in 1894) – that was to provide the basis of what became known as the 'Triple Entente'. Russia was also aligned with Serbia – and Serbia's very survival was threatened by Austria-Hungary. The twin-monarchy was allied directly with Germany, the product of a treaty from 1879. Following long-term enmity with France, a nation still brooding from its failure in the Franco-Prussian War of 1870–71, and the subsequent loss of Alsace-Lorraine, Germany had pre-prepared plans to tackle both France and its ally Russia, if so required. France was to be disposed of first, before dealing with the crushing might available in the vast territory of Russia. The plan, drawn up by Count von Schlieffen, required the neutrality and sovereignty of Belgium to be ignored. When this ponderous plan was enacted on 4 August 1914, Britain's direct involvement was assured. The Treaty of London (1839) guaranteed Belgian neutrality; with its borders slighted, and France threatened, Britain was to follow the other powers in declaring war, against Germany and Austria, on 4 August 1914. This treaty was the 'scrap of paper' often referred to in the literature of the day – and on postcards. Other allies would follow: Japan, tied by treaty in 1902 to help Britain in time of war, was to be a loyal ally; Italy, swayed by the promise of territorial expansion away from its former German and Austrian allies, was to join in 1915. The USA would follow in 1917, following the loss of the *Lusitania* in 1915 and the period of unrestricted submarine warfare, with many other nations joining the conflict as the defeat of the Central Powers seemed certain.

With Britain committed to war, many postcards were produced that emphasised the solidarity of the Allied nations – mostly European at this stage, but including Japan. Unfamiliar flags were particularly favoured, decorating a wide range of wares that sought to familiarise the public with the national flags of the

'A wee scrap o' paper is Britain's bond', a reference to the Treaty of London, guaranteeing Belgium's autonomy. Card published by Dobson, Molle & Co. of Edinburgh. The sender, a soldier in December 1914, drew comparison between himself and the picture.

A WEE "SCRAP O' PAPER" IS BRITAIN'S BOND.   No. 7

French postcards, heavy with sentiment, and illustrating the solidarity of the Allies 'against the Boches' (a derogatory term for the Germans). Both cards were sent home by soldiers serving in France.

Allies. Flags were used extensively on the cheaply produced crested china souvenirs that typify the late Victorian and Edwardian periods. They were also used widely on postcards, the number of flags growing throughout the war, new allies sensing an opportunity as the Central Powers faltered. 'Flag' cards were produced by many firms: by Millar & Lang of Glasgow, who before the war had fiercely opposed German imports of printed cards, and by the famous J. Salmon & Co. of Sevenoaks.

Postcards of the Allies published by A. Vivian Mansell & Co. Both were sent home by soldiers serving overseas.

In France, Britain's support for her Allies was often represented in florid terms dripping with sentiment; somewhat unrealistically uniformed Allies were represented arm-in-arm in battle, at home and facing the enemy. Though perhaps a little syrupy for the average British soldier, such cards were, nevertheless, bought and sent home from France. British-produced cards published by A. Vivian Mansell & Co. depicted the fighting men of all the Allied nations in stylised but perhaps more realistic terms. That this was acceptable to the fighting men is

Striking image of Britannia and her 'loyal hearts' published by William Ritchie & Sons of Edinburgh.

Illustrative of Britain's naval might – three 'super-dreadnoughts' illustrated on a card published by Valentines.

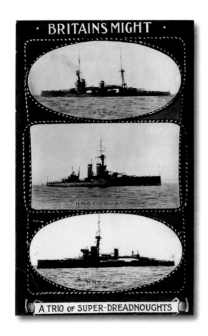

underlined by the fact that both of the cards illustrated on the previous page were sent by soldiers from overseas (France and Salonika) in 1917.

Important to the British war effort was the opinion of the Empire dominions. Britain's Empire was to provide millions of men for the fighting arms. Usually portrayed as the result of patriotic duty to serve the 'mother country', men and women from Canada, Australia, New Zealand, India and the African territories flocked to the cause. This loyalty was meat and drink to the postcard industry, which produced myriad cards designed to bolster British confidence in the might of its armies from across the Empire.

MILITARY MIGHT

With the opening of war, military subjects came to be popular with the public. To most people, the strength of the United Kingdom lay with its navy, a navy that had defended its shores for centuries, and that proved to be one of the most significant drivers in the development of the British Empire. The average Briton was justly proud of its navy, which in 1914 was the strongest in the world. As such, naval subjects, particularly of the capital ships of the Grand Fleet, were popular.

Most ships of the Royal Navy were destined to serve in the Grand Fleet, which at the very least acted as a major deterrent to German naval ambitions, and a defender of the homeland. The launch of HMS *Dreadnought* in 1906 was to challenge the superiority of other navies, including the developing German one, the Kaiser's 'pet project'. The escalation of the naval 'arms race' between Britain and Germany is seen as one of the most significant drivers to war. There is some irony, therefore, that the naval actions of both nations would depend very much on smaller ships and submarines while, apart from some major engagements (particularly

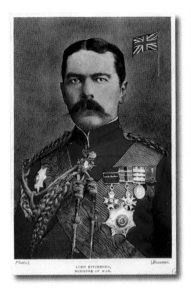

Far left: Bas-relief postcard of Kitchener, Minister of War, published in full colour by Scopes & Co. of Ipswich.

Left: Bas-relief postcard of Jellicoe, Admiral of the Fleet, also published by Scopes & Co. of Ipswich.

at Jutland, in 1916), the large fleets kept their distance – and naval reservists would be transformed into the soldiers of the Royal Naval Division.

Nevertheless, capital ships like *Dreadnought* and its successors were extremely popular subjects for postcards. Illustrated is a card published by Valentines (in the first rank of postcard publishers), with three 'super-dreadnoughts' of the British fleet, HMS *Neptune*, HMS *King George V* and HMS *Colossus*. All three fought with distinction at Jutland in 1916. In fact, naval engagements in the First World War were unsatisfactory affairs for those looking for good news. Jutland was a technical victory for the Grand Fleet, despite the heavy losses; the Dardanelles campaign of 1915 was rather more ignominious, with the Mediterranean Fleet driven back by minefields. A series of cards celebrates their actions, nonetheless.

In addition to ships of the line, military figures – the so-called 'Men of the Moment', generals, admirals and the like – made good postcard subjects. In the early war period, Field Marshal Sir John French, Commander-in-Chief of the British Expeditionary Force (BEF), was a popular figure, as was the ramrod-straight and luxuriantly moustachioed figure of another Field Marshal – Lord Kitchener. Kitchener was called to Government as Secretary of State for War in 1914. Bas-relief was a technique used to give extra dimension to the cards, and a magnificent example of Kitchener himself is illustrated, in a postcard published by Scopes & Co. of Ipswich – a manufacturer who specialised in the technique – as well as an example depicting Admiral Sir John Jellicoe, who commanded the Grand Fleet from the outbreak of war, and who was to command it in action at the Battle of

Right: One of a series of cards based on portraits of leading generals by war artist Francis Dodd.

GENERALS OF THE BRITISH ARMY.   Portraits by Francis Dodd.

Lieut.-General SIR H. E. WATTS,
K.C.B., C.M.G.,

who commanded the famous 7th Division in the Battle of the Somme, when it captured Mametz and Bazentin le Petit.

Below left: 'Gott Strafe this barbed wire', a card by Bruce Bairnsfather poking fun at the German phrase, 'Gott strafe England'.

Below right: The German sausage was an easy target for ridicule. Postcard published by J. Salmon.

Jutland. (Bas-relief cards were to have only a few words written on them to avoid postage penalties.) Cards depicting military and naval leaders continued in their popularity throughout the war. Rightly celebrated is the series of cards 'Generals of the British Army' from 1916, depicting drawings with colour wash by official war artist Francis Dodd. Dodd was appointed to this role by Charles Masterman, head of the War Propaganda Bureau. He produced this work while on the Western Front, making drawings of over thirty senior officers. A similar series from 1917, also by Dodd, covered the admirals.

MOCKING GERMANY

From the beginning, anti-German feeling was stirred up by the stories of atrocities in Belgium. Though some of these were greatly exaggerated – such as the mutilation of nuns and the bayoneting of babies – there were summary executions of civilians in

Bystander copyright.   "GOTT STRAFE THIS BARBED WIRE"

In Memoriam.

Goot gracious me ! Here
kom der British.

If der 1st Life Guards
haf gone by, den I kan kom

Goot gracious me ! Here
kom der Wilts. Yeomanry

Hurrah for the
11th YORKS

For gootness sake Halt !
der King's Own
are koming.

For gootness sake go back Here kom
der ROYAL ENGINEERS.

Range of cards by J. Salmon and E. Mack projecting Germans as buffoons; the format of these cards meant that there is an almost infinite variety of units used in the caption.

several towns and cities. On a wave of patriotic sympathy for the plight of 'plucky little Belgium', fuelled by the propaganda, German citizens and their businesses were attacked across Britain, and the German character openly mocked. Even the humble German sausage was a target for ridicule. Most critical were the fierce political cartoons of Dutchman Louis Raemakers, published in Britain in the magazine *Land and Water*. Brutal and dark, it is difficult to assess how popular the postcard versions of these illustrations were. In a similar vein, Germany proclaimed its hatred of Britain through its 'hymn of hate', written in 1914 by Ernst Lissauer, which proclaimed 'You we shall hate with enduring hate; …We have one foe, and one alone – ENGLAND!' As if this wasn't enough, Lissauer was also author of the slogan *Gott strafe England* ('God punish England') that became popular throughout Germany; the British would adopt it, tinged with ironic intent, and the term '*strafe*' would see wide currency on postcards.

For the most part, cartoons depicting the Germans as brutish, stupid and lumpish characters were most prevalent and popular in Britain; the Kaiser and his son ('Little Willie') would also be picked out for open mockery. A series produced by J. Salmon of Sevenoaks (in association with Eric Mack of London) illustrates German buffoons in full flight, with the variable slogan 'Goot gracious me! Here kom the British', usually altered to encompass a relevant regiment. No doubt popular mementoes of service, the truth would be somewhat different in the field.

Images of children were often used as a recruiting device. These cards were published by W. & K. of London (*left*), and Inter-Art (*right*).

RECRUITMENT

With the abrupt arrival of war in August 1914, it was clear that if Britain were to honour her commitments by fielding an army on the continent of Europe, then something more than the 300,000 or so men of the regular armies would be needed. Regular soldiers were recalled from leave; Reservists recalled to duty; Territorials called to the colours; and the ordinary civilian inspired by the spirit of the nation to join his country's forces. Strong leadership was also required: Earl Kitchener, a career soldier and national hero was appointed as Secretary of State for War. It was clear to Kitchener that the war would last at least three years, and he required more men to bolster the ranks of the Regulars. Within the first month of war, he appealed directly to the man in the street to join the New Army, an appeal

"THIS LITTLE PIG STAYED AT HOME"

ANOTHER 100,000 MEN WANTED

I'M SURE THEY OUGHT TO JOIN!

that would delve deeply into the sense of duty and patriotism that was prevalent at this potent time of Britain's history.

The flow of recruits in the first flush of the war overwhelmed the authorities. This flow was to continue almost unabated throughout 1914 and into 1915, and keeping up the pressure were the recruitment posters, which sprang up everywhere, using all kinds of devices to appeal to a myriad of emotions: 'Women of Britain say "Go!"', 'Daddy, what did you do in the Great War?', and 'Britons, Your Country Needs You!' Commercial postcards also played on the consciences of those not yet in uniform, usually subtly, and often using the device of children in uniform – a well-tried method of promoting guilt in a recipient not already in the armed forces. While white feathers were given out in the street to those not in uniform, so some postcards were used as a means of delivering the same message to the doorstep. Usually, such cards were homemade, crude and as shocking as any blackmail note. They are extremely rare today.

New recruitment opportunities to add men to the ever-widening fold were actively sought. The music hall was one of the most popular forms of popular entertainment in the pre-war and wartime years, and its stars were household names. With the glamour of the musical hall came the clamour to use it as a recruiting platform, and among many who joined the plea for more

Vesta Tilley, 'Britain's best recruiting sergeant', in costume.

men was male impersonator Vesta Tilley. Born Matilda Alice Pownes in 1864, Tilley was to become famous for the recruitment drives she organised. She was extraordinarily successful, dressing in a variety of uniforms to put her point across and earning herself the nickname 'Britain's best recruiting sergeant'. Her act was to evolve as the war progressed, and photographic postcards of her in uniform display this transition. She would be honoured in 1919 for her services to the war effort.

Despite the many pressures on men to join, the flow of recruits was to slow steadily throughout the war, particularly as the scale of the casualties became known. In an effort to avoid conscription, the Government appointed the dynamic Lord Derby as Director of Recruitment. He was to introduce the Derby Scheme, which encouraged voluntary 'attestation', on the understanding that the volunteer would not be called forward to the army (or navy) until there was an absolute requirement. 'Derby Men' would wear an armband indicating their willingness to serve – intended to keep the 'white feather vigilantes' at bay; the postcard illustrated below, by famous comic artist Fred Spurgin, is one of many produced from this time. It was published by the Art & Humour Publishing Co., a company set up by Fred's brother Maurice in 1915 to benefit from the wartime abandonment of German imports.

Ultimately, the Derby Scheme was an outright failure; all British citizens had been required to register for a National Identity Card in 1915, and it was clear from the data collected just how many men had still not presented themselves for military service. Putting aside those who were conscientious objectors, nearly 40 per cent of single men (and over 50 per cent of married men) not already in the services or in reserved occupations still failed to come forward. There was no choice but to introduce conscription, and following the introduction of the Military Service Act of 1916 all men aged 18–41 were called forward to a board to determine their military fitness. Some men were identified with stars on their National Registration documentation; their work was vital to the war effort. 'Starred Men' would wear a special lapel badge, and carry an entitling certificate of exemption from military service. For the others, being classified between A1 and C4 meant some form of military service, at home and abroad. Quick to capitalise on the comic opportunities provided by the call-up was the firm of James Bamforth of Holmfirth near Huddersfield. Producer of many comic cards,

The Derby Scheme provided the protection of an armband from the attentions of women intent on issuing white feathers to men not in uniform. This card by Fred Spurgin makes a pun on the numbers of men joining the scheme in 1915.

HELPING TO SWELL THE FIGURES?

FRED SPURGIN

Bamforth's 'Comic' and 'Witty' series illustrated hatchet-faced wives forcing their downtrodden men, rejected by the army as unfit, to take an active part in the housework – the implication being that this was a fate worse than serving on the Western Front. The facts were very plain – it was not.

Three cards published by Bamforth's from their 'Comic' and 'Witty' series that make reference to conscription, introduced in 1916.

"Ah, but you must be hardened to the cold, Mr Scotchman — I never leave mine off 'till July!"

"FULL MARCHING ORDER"
WHAT YOUR KIT FEELS LIKE
AFTER TEN MILES!

"Please, can you tell me the way to the 'Soldiers' Rest'?"
"'Soldiers' Rest'! Bless yer, mate— they don't get any!!!"

2286

"I love the life, but Oh you Kit!"

PREPARING FOR WAR

IN THE EARLY WAR PERIOD, following Lord Kitchener's famous appeal, men flocked to the colours. The first of these were to join new battalions of the county regiments – the so-called service battalions, otherwise known as 'Kitchener's Army'. To bulk the army more, spirited public figures raised whole battalions of men that were offered en masse to Kitchener to serve with the colours. These were usually referred to as the 'Pals' Battalions' – after Lord Derby's initiative in Liverpool, the first of its kind, recruiting bodies of men joining together from the same social class and workplace. Almost private armies, these battalions were clothed, fed and equipped from the purses of wealthy and influential people, before the War Office was prepared to take over their establishment as Service Battalions of His Majesty's Army.

The initial volunteers would serve in the Regular battalions and see action soon enough; the locally raised units would be trained together and be deployed *en masse* in the great offensive on the Somme in July 1916 – the losses from this action (57,500 casualties from the first day alone) shocking a nation already in mourning from the toll of 1915. These men would serve on all battle fronts, and by the end of the war, the few survivors would form the core of 'old sweats', reinforced by the conscripts of 1916 onwards. With so many men in uniform, the atmosphere of the early war period is captured in contemporary postcards. These often make direct reference to Kitchener's volunteers, and usually portray life in pre-Somme Britain as bright and breezy, an open-air, healthy life of huge army camps packed with fit young men. At this time, men in uniform were a hit with the ladies (particularly with the 'white feather brigade' of militant women frowning upon liaisons with men in civilian clothes) and postcards capitalised upon this theme too, while separation from loved ones provided plenty of opportunity for cards loaded with meaning.

The raw recruits of 1914–15 would all require training; coming from all walks of life, the freshly minted soldiers would often be unfit, undernourished and unskilled. It was the army's job to ensure that these men would be shaped

Opposite:
Four cards representative of the genius of Donald McGill in illustrating the life of the early war recruit in the training camps (see page 23). These cards were published by the International Art Company (Inter-Art).

into something that could take on the might of the professional German army that opposed them. On first joining, many new recruits were without anywhere to go other than home; the army had been overwhelmed with the numbers of men who volunteered. Gradually, new hutted camps were built across the country, camps that would eventually see thousands of men pass through their gates on the way to fronts in all parts of Europe, and beyond. All these aspects would find their way into the postcards of the period.

KITCHENER'S ARMY

The first recruits to join Kitchener's Army were forced to make compromises; there was little in the way of equipment, no uniforms, and no barracks. Lapel badges stood in for uniforms, and men 'went to war' training in flat caps and tweed suits and carrying broom handles. As a stopgap, simple uniforms were supplied in what has become known as 'Kitchener Blue' – blue serge in place of khaki. Soldiers in Kitchener Blue were to be photographed in uniform up and down the country, by photographers grateful for the new commercial opportunities that presented themselves. Their subjects often look awkward, conscious that they were not in regulation khaki; yet these pictures represent a snapshot of the pre-Somme citizen army frozen in time. Kitchener Blue varied widely in design, from standard uniforms made up in blue serge, through to the plain, pocketless variety reputedly surplus to requirements from the General Post Office. Issued with a forage cap, insignia would be variable, often extemporised. Contemporary postcard photographs of Kitchener men (like those illustrated) with quaint blue uniforms, khaki puttees and service boots are at odds with the images of men in the trenches we have come to associate with the First World War.

Two recruits in 'Kitchener Blue', the emergency uniforms issued in lieu of khaki in the early days of the war.

No new regiments (other than specialist corps) would be raised for Kitchener's Men; instead, they would be formed up in new 'service' battalions that would be added to the long-standing regiments of the British Army. The regiment has always been the source of pride within the British Army. Imbued with centuries of tradition, men assimilated into its ranks would take the weight of the regimental history onto their shoulders. Though soldiers would actually serve in one of its many battalions, some of them weeks old, it was expected that the traditions of the

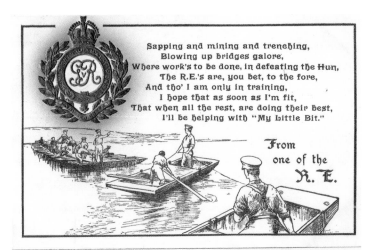

Regimental cards published by Birn Brothers Ltd of London, featuring a gold-embossed cap badge.

regiment would be maintained by these new recruits. Regimental cards had become popular in the Boer War, with colourful uniforms and the dash and verve of individuals in historic battles figuring strongly. The cap badge, loaded with symbolism and bearing regimental mottos and battle honours, was to be worn by all new soldiers – and avidly collected by small children from camp gates. Many postcards were produced to exploit this; some of the most attractive were produced by Birn Brothers Ltd of Bunhill Row in London. These were embossed with the regimental badge in gold, a sketch of the soldiers in action and a verse that explained the role of the regiment or corps. Always finishing with the phrase, 'From one of the ...', these cards served as a reminder that the sender was 'doing his bit'.

IN THE CAMPS

Camps were set up across the country to house the vast influx of new recruits to the armed forces. For the Leeds Pals, raised and funded by the Corporation and Mayor of Leeds, there was a need for a new camp, constructed on the Pennine fells that surrounded the city; the same is true of many of the other 'city battalions' of the industrial conurbations of Britain. Many other camps were erected around the country; they would become part of the local geography, and photographic postcards were sold indicating their growing prominence in the landscape.

Alongside the photographic cards, a plethora of humorous cards invariably stressed the camp routine or conditions – those illustrated below are typical. Often these would take the form of a text card, usually with verse, that would explain the routine of camp life. In others, this routine was displayed through humorous sketches, often drawn by Donald McGill and published mostly by the International Art Company (Inter-Art). Part of the long-

Two cards by Donald McGill, from Inter-Art's 'Recruits' series, which make direct reference to the newly-joined men of Kitchener's Army.

running 'Comique' series, these cards were picked up by recruits intending to illustrate the lighter side of their life in camp – with an underlying strong grain of truth. (The Navy would also be subjected to McGill's wit).

McGill is perhaps the most famous of all postcard artists, mostly because of his prolific output, his post-war fascination with 'saucy themes', and his brush with antiquated 'decency' laws in the 1950s, at the age of 80 – which saw him fined £50 for his brand of innuendo. Born in London in 1875, he became a naval draughtsman until his career in postcards began accidentally in 1904, after drawing a get-well card for a sick nephew; within a year this was to become his full-time occupation. Over his career McGill produced an estimated 12,000 designs, of which 200 million copies are thought to have been printed. McGill's wartime output is well observed and well drawn (though some commentators have sought to criticise his style as crude). Though not a military man, he captures accurately the mood of the pre-Somme army: the weight of the equipment, aspects of training, chores, trench digging and a multitude of other minor humorous incidents from camp life. That these cards would also cross the Channel is illustrated by some having French translations of their comic lines.

Yet of all the postcards produced of camp life early in the war, perhaps none captures the exuberance of the men more effectively than the 'Camp Silhouette Series' produced by postcard publisher Photochrom Ltd of London. Drawn by artist G. E. Shepheard, these cards uniquely illustrate the spirit of training in early-war Britain, from reveille to pay day, as a series of humorous silhouettes. Beautifully crafted, they express a time of innocent exuberance before the realisation of the true casualties of the war were felt. These cards would have a second lease of life in 1939–40. The camp routine depicted by these and other cards of the period was one of early to rise, early to bed, with the imposition of communal living in bell tents (designed to hold at least eight men, feet to the centre pole), or, for

Previous page below: Text cards like these were popular with men in the camps. Both Kinmell Park (in North Wales) and Clipstone Park (in Nottinghamshire) would house thousands of Kitchener's men.

Photochrom's 'Camp Silhouette Series' captures the spirit of the early-war camps.

23

Right: Novelty camp card produced by The Regent Publishing Co. of London. Rotating the soldier's hat reveals different expression in tune with three days' leave or six days' 'confined to barracks' (CB).

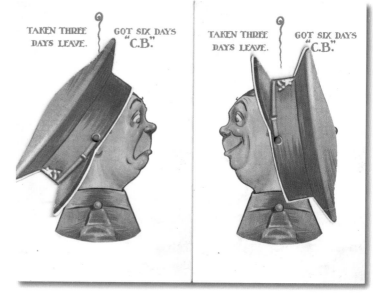

Below: Two soldiers of the Welsh Regiment pose in the same studio, with the same backdrop. In some cases, photographers would provide props that would jar with their subject.

the better off, timber-constructed huts. All would form the basis for the transition from civilian to soldier, prior to being named for a draft to the front line. As the war ground on, so these camps would be filled with conscripts, and with those soldiers unlucky enough to have been wounded and passed fit once again for front-line duty. Men of the camps would make their way to the Channel Ports before being sent overseas, and a further period of acclimatisation training closer to the actual theatres of war.

As in earlier wars, before departing for the front new soldiers were keen to record their appearance in uniform through a visit to a photographer's studio. In the nineteenth century, small, multiple photographic prints known as *cartes de visite* were obtained for distribution amongst friends and family. In the First World War, photography had moved forward such that the process created a negative, from which multiple copies of postcard-sized photographs – usually with a divided postcard back – could be obtained. Posed in standard studio sets, usually with an incongruous backdrop and piece of furniture for support, new soldiers would pose before setting off for the front. Often anonymous now, these images provide valuable insights into the life of the soldier in uniform. Other photos would be taken in the rest areas when the soldiers finally reached France. Sadly, many would remain uncollected.

Left: Women often dressed in their sweetheart's uniform for photographers, as a token of their love. Here four women have donned tunics and caps.

SWEETHEART CARDS

The separation felt by soldiers in training camps from their wives, sweethearts and loved ones was tangible, often depicted in postcards. In this more innocent age, postcards sent by these men were often used as a way of expressing feelings without recourse to emotionally charged words. Encountered are photographic cards of women in the caps or even uniforms of their men. Common also are 'Mizpah' cards – the term derived from a phrase in the Bible associated with separated loved ones – and forget-me-not cards. Usually sent from soldiers to their sweethearts, they are often found in verse, or with suitable illustrations emphasising separation. Produced by a wide variety of publishers, they are common today, perhaps none more so than the song cards created by James Bamforth.

Below: Separation from loved ones was a popular topic for postcard manufacturers, here by Harold Copping (the artist, left), and Wildt 'W&K', right.

Bamforth was a publishing company that specialised in the production of so-called 'song cards'; postcards with a saccharine-sweet message of love depicting doe-eyed girls and dreamy Tommies juxtaposed against the words of popular songs. Famously, the 'life models' used were all employees of Bamforth's factory in Holmfirth near Huddersfield. James Bamforth had set up his works to supply lantern slides illustrating the popular songs of the day – which were easily

Forget-me-not and 'Mizpah' cards are common mementoes of separation, and were produced by many publishers.

My Thoughts are of You.

At Brown Knoll Camp.——*A Soldier's Letter.*

As there hasn't been time for a letter to-day,
I am sending this card to say things are all gay.
But with drilling and marching, the day is soon done,
And we're so much more tired than when we begun.

Still I'm keeping quite happy, and jolly well fit,
And am glad, after all, to be doing my bit.
But throughout the whole day, little girlie so true,
Believe me, my thoughts dear, are only of YOU.

Now we don't mind the training, we're out for a win,
And we mustn't fall out in the March to Berlin !
We are keeping the Old Union Jack floating free,
Thanks to Kitchener's judgment, the Army and—ME

When Peace comes again, and I'm once more at home,
We'll take the same walks where we oft used to roam ;
So write soon, my dearie, to your Soldier Boy, who,
Through the long day has *Thoughts Only of YOU.*

From H. Hunt 8th Manchesters.

A Soldier's Letter to his SWEETHEART.

From GMH ♡

" THINKING OF YOU."

MIZPAH.

" May the LORD watch between thee and me when we are absent one from another."

Sweetheart, when the day's work is over,
And from drilling I am free ;
Sitting around the old camp fire,
My thoughts are ALL of thee.
I'm not much good with a pen, dear,
For the gun is now my line ;
So I send you *Fond Love* by this Postcard,
As I thought perhaps you might pine.
When Old England's Cry for soldiers,
Sounded through our dear homeland ;
'Twas Duty's Call—and I obeyed it,
I *knew* that *you* would understand.
As I sit here fondly dreaming,
I picture your sweet dear face ;
Helping, cheering on the weary,
Round about the dear old place.
Our ''Boys'' are doing well, dear,
For we're always " On the go '' ;
" Forming Fours " and Swedish Drill,
" Getting Fit '' to thrash the Foe.
Thoughts of *YOU* come flocking to me,
Gives me bliss—without alloy ;
Looking forward to a future,
Peaceful future—full of joy.

Copyri

FONDEST LOVE FROM THE CAMP.

To my Dear Little " Chicks."

A Soldier's Verse Letter to his children.

My dear little Chicks I'm thinking of YOU,
And dear Mother throughout the long day ;
And wonder at times how you're getting on,
While your Daddy's so far away.

Now, be good children, and don't worry Mummy,
Then when I come home again on " leave ;"
My " Kit Bag " I'll fill with Toys and Good Things,
Like Santa Claus on Christmas Eve.

Now, tell dear Mummy, I'd like to have,
A photo of you all—as you are ;
Just to cheer me up while " doing my bit."
Though the distance between us is far.

I dreamt last night I was home again,
With you and Mother so dear ;
But at early dawn the Buglers blew
" *Reveille* " in tones loud and clear.

FORGET-ME-NOT, my thoughts are of YOU,
While marching or from drill set free ;
My loving thoughts for ever turn,
To Home—and Dear Ones—far from me.

From Dad " LONGING FOR YOU."

WHEN YOU COME HOME (4).

When we go home dear, when we go ho
No more to leave you, no more to roan
God will remember! God will provide!
When we go home at even-tide.

WHEN YOU COME HOME (1).
Birds in the garden, a l day long, singing for me their
happy song,
Flow'rs in the sunshine, wind and dew, all of them
speak to me of you;
You that I long for, near or far, you that I follow
like a star;
Day may be weary, weary and long, you will come
home at even-song.

transformed into a series of postcards. That these were popular with sweethearts is clear from the number and diversity of examples that are found today. For the most part, however, they were sent between sweethearts at home; Tommy, though often accused of being sentimental, was also a realist – and the early editions of these cards were certainly far detached from reality.

Bamforth's would also illustrate popular wartime tunes; such as 'Take Me Back to Dear Old Blighty'. Singing had always been associated with front-line troops, and the First World War is particularly remembered for the extent and diversity of its marching songs – 'It's a Long Way to Tipperary' being the most famous of them all. Written by Jack Judge and Harry Williams and published in 1912, the first recorded use of it in the war is credited to an Irish regiment, the Connaught Rangers, as they arrived in Boulogne in August 1914. It was to appear on several song cards.

James Bamforth specialised in sentimental 'song cards', the people pictured in the cards being employees at the factory in Holmfirth.

Dear Mother:
I am sending you 10/- —but not this week

'IN THE TRENCHES'

THE GREAT WAR is usually associated with 'war in the trenches'. Though trench warfare was by no means new – having surfaced in the American Civil War and the Russo-Japanese War, both then within living memory – the scale and longevity of trench warfare as developed in 1914–18 was to take the world by surprise. There were phases of open warfare, of course, at the beginning and end of the war on the Western Front in France and Flanders, as well as in the more open conditions of the Middle East. There was also the war at sea and in the air – both vital to the prosecution of the global conflict. But it was 'the trenches', and the army that manned them, that were to epitomise the war as it was depicted in contemporary postcards.

Life in the trenches was dominated by routine: the rhythm of daily existence, which commenced with the 'morning hate' at stand-to, an hour before dawn, through to its equivalent at dusk, when the soldiers would man the fire step in anticipation of attack. By day, sentries would be posted at box periscopes or their simple mirror equivalents, one per platoon, looking out for *minenwerfers*, gas and unusual activity. By night, sentries would stand nervously on the fire step, nervous of the casual and random play of a machine gun across no-man's-land. Between times, there would be inspections, trench repair and the issue of rations. In fact, it was the supply and issue of rations that had one of the greatest effects on morale in the front line, the supply of hot food being the most important. All too often, falling back on the standard rations of corned 'bully'

Opposite: Dudley Buxton's take on trench life, from Inter-Art's 'Comique' series.

Below: Postcard publishers were quick to latch onto 'the trenches', 'somewhere in France' as suitable subjects for cards.

29

Right: 'The Outpost', a late-war, cheaply produced card depicting life in the trenches.

THE OUTPOST
A British " Tommy " watching the enemy through his periscope

beef and biscuits — iron rations — was called for. Welcomed by many — but not by all — would be the issue of the rum ration, under close inspection of an officer. The fiery effect of this viscous liquid was a boon in the cold, damp conditions of the trench.

There was another rhythm to trench life, however. Men would rarely be at the front line for more than a week, and would spend at least another period in reserve trenches, ready to be called upon in case of emergency. A third week would see soldiers withdrawn on rest, to billets behind the front line. Home leave for the average soldier would be infrequent. These themes would be picked up by the postcard manufacturers; informed by soldier-artists, they produced cards that would in some way depict the conditions experienced at the front. Postcards depicting front-line life fall broadly into two categories: humorous cards, often drawn by soldiers themselves and thereby providing a direct link with the experience of the front line; and photographic cards produced in association with the official photographers.

Below: Given the difficult ground conditions in Flanders, trenches were often flooded, as depicted in this well-observed humorous card.

I WONDER WHEN THE BLINKIN' TIDE GOES OUT TED.

PUTTING A BRAVE FACE ON IT
Humorous cards depicting the conditions of trench warfare often represent the authentic voice of the average soldier — particularly if the postcard artist was actually a soldier himself. One of the most accurate depictions of trench warfare is that published in a series of cards by Fergus Mackain, entitled *Sketches of Tommy's Life*. These postcards were published in Boulogne by Imprimérie P. Gaulthier, and subsequently by the Paris firm of Visé, in four separate series of nine cards each, together with a large number of lesser-known greetings cards in the same vein.

Mackain has a deftness of touch in his charming and understated colour-washed cards. The *Sketches* themselves fall into four chapters of Tommy's life: 'In Training'; 'At the Base'; 'Up the Line' and 'Out on Rest'.

Two cards from Fergus Mackain's 'Sketches of Tommy's Life': (above left) Series 1: 'In Training'; (above right) Series 2: 'At the Base'.

Humorous aspects are present, of course, but underlying the cards is a deep understanding of what it was like to be a soldier on the Western Front. The soldier's kit is reproduced with minute detail: trench periscopes, bully beef tins, clasp knives, rifle pull-throughs, washing kit holdalls, and so on. These essential yet seemingly mundane items are reproduced in the background to the cards, and reward detailed inspection. Situations are apt, too: the seemingly endless issue of kit items; housey-housey at the base; issue of the rum ration and scanning the sky for trench mortars, whistle in hand in the trenches; ablutions in the reserve trenches – all are handled with an intimate understanding derived from direct experience.

This is understandable; after all, 4249 Private Fergus H. E. Mackain served with the 23rd (1st Sportsman's) Battalion Royal Fusiliers on the Western Front. The Sportsman's battalion was raised in the autumn of 1914 by Mrs Cunliffe-Owen, a society lady sufficiently well-connected to be able to telegraph Lord Kitchener with the question, 'Will you accept complete battalion of upper and middle class men, physically fit, able to shoot and ride, up to the age of 45?' She was to receive the answer 'Lord Kitchener gratefully accepts complete battalion'. This influential lady finally handed over the battalion to the army in April 1915. The 23rd Battalion was to serve in the 99th Brigade throughout the war, with 4,987 officers and men serving, and 3,241 as casualties – killed, wounded and missing. Mackain survived the war, serving with the battalion as a private. He was to be transferred to the Army Service Corps later in the war – usual with men who had suffered wounds and illness.

Below: Greetings cards by Fergus Mackain, depicting front-line life.

I've got a cushy job now!

Sorry! but I must not let you know whereabouts I am in France!

Mackain's story is not unusual, and his life as a private soldier undistinguished; but his cards are unique not simply because they illustrate the life of the average 'Tommy' in extraordinary detail – many other artists, like Bairnsfather, can claim that too – but also that they were published in Boulogne, and were therefore sent home by ordinary soldiers on active service. His cards often have Field Post Office stamps, and messages that draw attention to the similarities between the soldiers depicted on the cards and the soldier sending the cards home. In this way Mackain's cards act as a window on what life must have been like for the average soldier at the Front, and are authentic documents of life in the Great War. Yet overshadowing Mackain's work is that of a serving officer, Captain Bruce Bairnsfather, and his *Fragments from France*.

Fragments from France: accurate depictions of front-line life by serving officer, Captain Bruce Bairnsfather, and published in *The Bystander*.

Bairnsfather was an officer, a subaltern, who left for war in the autumn of 1914 with his men of the 1st Battalion of the Royal Warwickshire Regiment. Destined to serve his time in the mud of the southern part of the Ypres Salient, close to Ploegsteert ('Plugstreet') Wood, he was to use skills honed at Hassell's School of Commercial Art by drawing cartoons depicting the life of the soldier in the trenches of 1914–15 that resonated with the men themselves. According to legend – and as described in his account of this time, *Bullets and Billets* – his first cartoons were drawn on the walls of the ruined rural buildings in the area. Destined to be published by the popular illustrated magazine *The Bystander*, Bairnsfather's *Fragments from France* would be an immediate hit with the public, popular with both civilian and soldier alike in depicting aspects of life in the trenches that would be otherwise difficult to discern from the press. In fact, Bruce Bairnsfather's cartoons were a hit with almost everyone, excepting perhaps those in high positions who deplored the 'base language' and scruffiness of the front-line soldier depicted.

Bairnsfather was to become a celebrity, the power of his cartoons sufficient for him to be promoted to captain, and be withdrawn from the front line to take on the role of 'officer cartoonist' – a morale-boosting liaison role. His creation, Old Bill – a wise 'old contemptible', 'out since Mons' – was also to attain celebrity status, largely through his unbendingly stoic – and sardonic – approach to the trials of front-line life. The drawings: 'Well if you knows of a better 'ole, go to it', and 'At present we are staying at a farm...' are classic understatements of the real hardships of the trenches. As well as appearing in *The Bystander*, Bairnsfather's collected drawings were published in a series of eight *Fragments from France* magazines from January 1916 to 1919. Postcards would soon follow, and a total of fifty-four were issued – in nine packets of six, each with its own envelope, from May 1916. Like the magazines themselves, they were an instant hit. Published at home, few Bairnsfather cards were sent by soldiers serving overseas, but most would agree that Old Bill's unique brand of humour typified that of the British soldier himself.

Perhaps following the lead set up by the likes of Bairnsfather and Mackain, the popularity of the depiction of soldiers in the front line meant that a whole range of humorous cards – some of dubious quality –

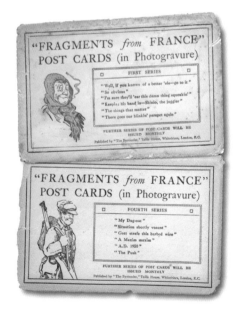

Surviving envelopes from Bairnsfather's *Fragments from France* postcards. Each one contained a series of eight different cards.

Examples of cards produced by soldier artists: 'Military Terms – Illustrated' series by 'Will. J. Woodall, B.E.F.', and depictions of the trials of life in the artillery by Reg Carter of the RFA.

were to appear that dealt with front-line life. Some were out-and-out imitators of the Bairnsfather style – crude and unsigned, they were designed to cash in on the money-spinning phenomenon. Others were more original: while Donald McGill rarely strayed overseas with his comic creations, a fellow artist at International Art Company, Dudley Buxton, turned his hand to front-line life with some success. Talented soldier-artists would also turn their hand to the depiction of their life at the front; usually reproduced from line drawings, these included the 'Military Terms – Illustrated' series signed 'Will. J. Woodall, B.E.F.' (there are at least four soldiers with this name who served in the BEF), and depictions of the trials of life in the artillery by Reg Carter of the Royal Field Artillery (RFA).

Every aspect was covered. An interesting series published by Millar & Lang is that depicting 'Tommy's French'. Thrown into a new country, Tommy quickly picked up enough French to get by, just as he had in India as a pre-war regular. A variety of pidgin French was soon developed, despite the efforts of the authorities to encourage proficiency. 'Napoo' was a particular favourite, meaning no more, finished, broken, worn out, or useless – it was derived from *il n'y en a plus* (there is no more). 'No compree' – derived from *compris* – which meant that there was no understanding on either side, was also common. Adoption of pidgin French was therefore inevitable.

PHOTOGRAPHIC SERIES

If humorous cards came close to capturing the essence of the everyday life of a soldier, then it was the various photographic series produced at home that went a long way in depicting the landscape of battle. First in this line were the distinctive 'On Active Service' cards produced in 1914 by Photochrom Ltd. Issued in sets of twenty-four at a time, these distinctive, partially colourised photographs were set in a yellow-orange border. The photographs were claimed to be 'copyright photographs from the front', some of which were attributed to the *Daily Mail*. Most of the images relate to actions from 1914 to 1915 and depict life 'in the air, on land and at sea' in France, Belgium and the Dardanelles.

Cards illustrating the adoption of 'pidgin French' by British soldiers.

Left: 'On Active Service' photographic cards, produced by Photochrom Ltd.

Below: 'The Dardanelles Campaign' cards produced by Raphael Tuck.

The Gallipoli Campaign of 1915 was the particular subject of another set of cards – 'The Dardanelles Operation' – which reproduced official photographs of the campaign at sea and on land. These were published by Raphael Tuck & Sons, a company usually associated with high quality, and this is especially true of this series. Printed in high quality sepia through the photogravure process (involving reproduction of photographs by mechanical plate-etching), these cards reproduce some of the best-known official photographs of the campaign in several series, all accompanied by extensive captions.

The most widespread photographic cards by far, however, were those published by the *Daily Mail*. Issued in sets of eight cards, each set was sold in packets for the princely sum of sixpence. In total

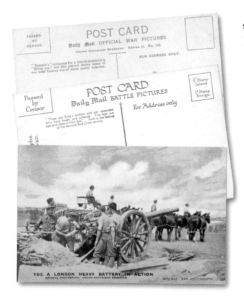

Daily Mail Battle Pictures.

some twenty-two series of '*Daily Mail* Battle Pictures' were issued, with millions of cards produced overall. The source of the images came from the official photographers, a call for tenders to reproduce the images having been made by the Press Bureau in 1916. The *Daily Mail* is reputed to have paid a minimum of £5,000 for the right to reproduce the pictures, with half of the net profits going to service charities.

The cards were issued in three formats: colour, sepia (photogravure) and photographic facsimile. The first three series, issued at the end of September 1916, were reproduced in colour; the next three, in photogravure; four more, in photographic facsimile and so on. The cards varied in title from 'Battle Pictures' to 'War Pictures' and then 'War Postcards'. Special themes were also explored – Series XI and XII illustrated in colour, and then again in photogravure, the visit of King George V 'to the Front'. Series XIII–XV depicted various aspects of the war on the Western Front in colour, and the same cards were repeated in Series XVI–XVIII in sepia tone. This repetition was a commercial response to the collecting craze that followed the release of the cards; demand was intense, and the variation was intended to cater for all tastes. Special albums were issued, titled '*Daily Mail* Official War Postcards' in October 1916; retailing at two shillings and sixpence, they were designed to hold 240 cards (176 were produced in all). From Series XVI onwards the cards appeared only in sepia-toned photogravure; special sets included 'Anzacs in France' (Series XIX and XX), and the final series, issued in April 1917, depicting the stages of an attack (Series XXII). The success of the cards overall was in their depiction of all aspects of trench warfare on the Western Front.

Album produced by the *Daily Mail* to house its twenty-two sets of Battle Pictures postcards.

With the *Daily Mail* managing a spectacular coup with the issue of its War Postcards, not to be outdone, its rival, the illustrated tabloid the *Daily Mirror*, negotiated a deal with the Canadian authorities to issue its own, equally stunning brand of photographic

postcards. Like the *Daily Mail* versions, these were issued in colour, photogravure and photographic versions, and were based on Canadian Official War Photographs. Other sets include the colour '*Tit-bits* War Pictures', produced in at least four series by the popular magazine; and another colour series based on French official photographs that was issued by Newspaper Illustrations Ltd. Several similar series were produced by other publishers. The relative scarcity of all of these cards is perhaps a testimony to the success of the *Daily Mail* War Pictures.

Above: *Daily Mirror* Canadian Official Pictures cards, produced to rival the *Daily Mail* output.

Left: *Tit-bits* War Pictures cards. *Tit-bits* was a popular illustrated magazine.

George Street
18 Peel
dstore

M. D'Vyley, I am just
Somewhere in Flanders and
have a long train
have a buil

Mrs J H Ma
90 Thorn
West
Lon

On Active Service
Carte Postale
8. 7. 16
Correspondance

Am getting along

O. A. S

a card hoping
ll find you well
n the same
dropping a
to Dick this
ing. I hope he
spend his Chris
at home with
e alf

A. H. KATZ

FIELD POST OFFICE

Mrs S. Ald
"Wo
G. Jra
Englan

G. Frase
CORRESPONDANCE

Miss. W. Glynn
Arial House
Princ

Miss L

LETTERS HOME

THE ROYAL ENGINEERS, that most versatile of all Corps of the British Army, was to play a pivotal role in keeping the soldiers in touch with their home life, through its postal service. This had been set up in 1913, with an initial establishment of ten officers and 290 other ranks, intended to support an Expeditionary Force of six divisions in time of war. In August 1914, the postal service moved to France with the army. Mail for the BEF from the United Kingdom was collected by the Post Office at home and sent to France, gathering at Le Havre, where the RE took over. The main unit was the Field Post Office (FPO). Although little more than an iron box and flag of office, it was to provide an essential service for the men of the BEF, Mediterranean Expeditionary Force (MEF) and other overseas forces throughout the war.

Letters to and from the front were of great importance in maintaining the morale of the troops. For soldiers, sailors and airmen, postal charges were abolished in 1914, and it was sufficient to write 'On Active Service' on the card or envelope to ensure its safe delivery on posting. Each card or letter would carry the postmark or cachet of the army field post office, each FPO having its own number and special cachet mark – of which there is a bewildering array, of great interest to postal historians today. An officer would censor each piece of correspondence, striking through offending passages with a blue pencil. Typical 'offences' would be references to current locations, defences, offensives or casualties. In response, card writers would go to great lengths to set up a code system, perhaps using capital letters of consecutive sentences to spell out a place.

While the responsibility of the Army Postal Section was ensuring that these letters reached home safely, it was also their job to make sure that letters and parcels arriving for the troops were delivered – an often difficult task given the movement of troops to and from the trenches, on many different action fronts. The speed of delivery varied, but was often next-day to the Western Front. Often, poignantly, letters would arrive for soldiers recently killed; they were returned to their sender with the cachet 'killed in action' or 'deceased', stark reminders of the fortunes of war.

Opposite:
Field censor marks. From 1914 these were the circle and square; 1915, the triangle; 1916, hexagonal and oval; 1917, rectangular. Octagonal stamps (1917) were only for Egypt and Salonika; shield shapes (1918), from Italy.

Cards posted by an officer from Rouen, bearing the cachet 'Army Base Post Office 2', and triangular field censor mark. He writes: 'Somewhere in Flanders...The Colonel is topping'.

YMCA postcard; stationery could be purchased from YMCA and Church Army huts both at home and overseas.

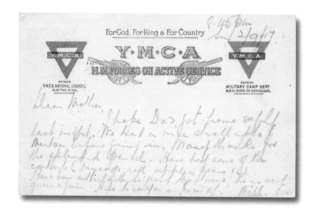

FIELD SERVICE POSTCARDS

Stationery used by the troops was provided from many sources – bought locally in shops in the base or rear areas, supplied from home, obtained from the many YMCA and Church Army huts (charities providing basic comforts for the troops), or gathered from 'comforts funds' set up at home. Often these were letters or letter cards; but for some soldiers, the maintenance of a normal level of correspondence was trying. Postcards were easier to write and quick to send. This was especially so for the humble Field Service Postcard, which was a means of getting a simple message home without having to go to the trouble of writing a long letter. Supplied by the military authorities (often in advance of

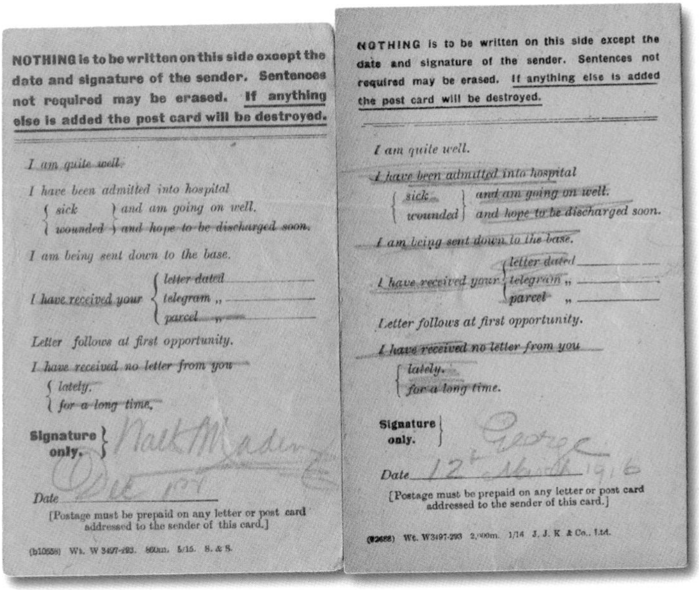

NOTHING is to be written on this side except the date and signature of the sender. Sentences not required may be erased. If anything else is added the post card will be destroyed.

I am quite well.

I have been admitted into hospital

{ *sick* } *and am going on well.*
{ *wounded* } *and hope to be discharged soon.*

I am being sent down to the base.

I have received your { *letter dated* _____
{ *telegram ,, * _____
{ *parcel ,,* _____

Letter follows at first opportunity.

I have received no letter from you { *lately.*
{ *for a long time.*

Signature }
only. }

Date _____

[Postage must be prepaid on any letter or post card addressed to the sender of this card.]

NOTHING is to be written on this side except the date and signature of the sender. Sentences not required may be erased. If anything else is added the post card will be destroyed.

I am quite well.

I have been admitted into hospital

{ *sick* } *and am going on well.*
{ *wounded* } *and hope to be discharged soon.*

I am being sent down to the base.

I have received your { *letter dated* _____
{ *telegram ,, * _____
{ *parcel ,,* _____

Letter follows at first opportunity.

I have received no letter from you { *lately.*
{ *for a long time.*

Signature }
only. } *George*

Date *12 March 1916*

[Postage must be prepaid on any letter or post card addressed to the sender of this card.]

The Field Service Postcard was completed by crossing out the prepared sentences; apart from the soldier's name and the date of posting (and Christmas greetings), nothing else was allowed to be written on this side. A typical message is illustrated on the right; the card is from a sick soldier serving in Gallipoli.

offensives), all the sender had to do was cross out a few lines in order to get his message across, usually expressing the view that all was fine, and that 'letter follows at earliest opportunity'. Some provided more worry, however, with the sender in hospital, sick or wounded.

Millions of Field Service Postcards were sent (and parodied widely), and all the combatant nations were to have their own versions. For British Empire troops, various language versions were available for soldiers of the Indian Army, who first arrived in France in 1914. Some soldiers shied from sending them, fearing their buff colour and official format could be off-putting to the folks back home. For these men, locally-bought cards were favoured. The usual messages on these cards relate to the contents of parcels, or a reflection on the soldier's state of mind – 'In the pink' was usual.

Postcards sent from the battle zone are often simply topographical, usually associated with the rear and base areas, such as Rouen or Le Havre – though army censors still worked to strike out their captions. In other cases, they depicted beautiful girls, flowers or other incongruous images far from the thought of war. Their messages are most commonly simple and understated, with little reference to battle conditions – and deterred from doing so by the actions of the field censor. The range of stamps and marks on these cards has received extensive research, and their diversity is too great to illustrate here. As a guide, cards posted while at base, headquarters or in hospital usually carry the double ring cachet bearing the title 'Army Post Office' or 'Base Post Office'; those at Divisional or Brigade headquarters,

Nothing to be Written on this Card except the date and signature of Sender (if capable of signing his name) Sentences not required may be deleted and the recipient will be delighted.

I Am quite well (now that we are on shore).

I { Am / Am not / Am never } Going to Bed

I Have been { In the BRISTOL and all the Cafés

{ Sick but left it in the sea { Broke but hope to touch lucky

† Am being sent down the base (because I have not paid my sub's)

I Have received your { Eno's Blessing Curses

I Have received no money from you

{ Lately { For a long time

I Am still happy and cheerfull

Signature only

Date

LOVE'S SERVICE POST CARD

NOTHING is to be written on this side except crosses marked thus (x). You may take out any little thing that you please. If anything else is added, the meaning of this card will be destroyed.

I am A.1. and O.K. on the Q.T.

I have been admitted to be hospitable
  sick } with longing for you.
  wounded } if you don't write.

I am being sent down to embrace.

I have received { letters L-O-V-E. tell-a-crams (none). parcel of good cheer.

Let us follow at first opportunity—
  (your good example).

I have received no kisses from you
  { lately.
  { for a long time.

Signature only. } J. M. Ure Kidd

Date : any old time

FRED · SPURGIN ·

The Field Service Postcard was often parodied. The left-hand card was produced by a hotel for post-war battlefield visitors; the right-hand card was a wartime production.

or at rail heads, are usually marked 'Field Post Office'. There are at least 1,600 different stamps from all fronts operated by the British Army.

A much simpler guide is the shape of the cachet used by the army censor, with representative stamp types illustrated. The first ones, used by the British Expeditionary Force in France in 1914, were circular, and then square; in April 1915 this changed to a triangle (both squares and triangles were used extensively in the Mediterranean Theatre). A hexagonal design replaced this in January 1916; oval and then rectangular stamps followed in November 1916 and October 1917 respectively. These were not used outside France and Belgium. Finally, a distinctive octagonal stamp was produced for use in Egypt and Salonika in October 1917, and a shield design for use in Italy in April 1918. Commonly found on postcards sent from the front, these censor stamps give some indication of the theatre of war, of much interest to modern family historians.

Soldier portraits sent home from the front. All carry respirators.

SOUVENIRS FROM THE FRONT

As at home, photographers in the rear areas of all battle zones did a roaring trade in providing soldiers with photographic images of themselves – reproduced as postcards – as a souvenir of their service overseas. These differ from the photos taken at home: for one thing, the soldiers generally carry respirators, and for another, they usually bear the marks of war – dirty uniforms, muddy boots, miscellaneous equipment slung about their person. Finally, another tell-tale sign is that the postcard backs usually read 'Carte Postale', rather than the more humble 'Postcard'. For the most part, these were posed in studios, but the ruins of Belgium, France and other places were also popular.

Pin-ups, locally produced in France, were popular amongst some soldiers. They were usually discarded before action, in fear of them being sent home with personal effects if killed.

For soldiers in the rear areas, risqué postcards of semi-naked women, or of elegant girls from the magazine pages, were a draw. Fear of having these sent home with soldiers' effects if killed meant they were rarely kept for long. But by far the most important postcard souvenirs of front-line service are the silk postcards, a real

phenomenon of the war. Though first produced in 1907, the new market provided by the influx of soldiers saw them gain popularity early on in 1915, as the locals realised the potential for the marketing of their skills; some estimates suggest that as many as ten million cards were produced during the war. Each card was produced as part of a cottage industry which saw mostly women engaged in intricate designs being hand embroidered onto strips of silk mesh, the design being repeated as many as twenty-five times

Silk postcards 'from France', a phenomenon of the war. Those bearing regimental badges are most sought after.

on a strip, before being sent to a factory for cutting and mounting as postcards and greetings cards.

The cards themselves were bought from civilians trying to scrape a living from supplying the soldiers' needs in the immediate battle zone. They were not cheap, each one costing as much as three times the daily pay of the average soldier. Though true postcards, they were sold and sent home in simple envelopes intended to protect their precious contents. There is a huge range; sentimental messages – 'friendship', 'birthday greetings', 'Home Sweet Home' and so on were popular, and are commonest, as are cards celebrating festivals and holidays. Many had delicately opening pockets with a small card insert; others would give 'greetings from France' or poignant messages 'from the trenches'. But for many collectors, it is the cards with intricately worked regimental crests that are the most sought after.

Greetings 'from the trenches' – a rare silk postcard message. 'Flowers from France' was more typical of the genre.

CHRISTMAS CARDS

Christmas cards sent from the front line were to become one of many postal phenomena associated with the Great War. In 1914, most of the cards that were sent had been obtained from the rear areas, and were based on the commercial versions available, with commercially minded soldier artists like Mackain also producing cards. Very soon, silk cards were produced for festivals like Christmas, Easter and anniversaries. Specially drawn and commissioned cards, produced by individual divisions, brigades and battalions, also joined these. Based usually on a piece of art created by a soldier, they were printed locally and sent out in their hundreds. Collectable today, they usually depict a hapless enemy pursued by a plucky Tommy.

Right: Divisional Christmas cards, locally produced in the late war period.

Below: Locally produced Christmas cards from the Salonika front, printed by The Royal Engineers Surrey Company in Macedonia.

Those sent from the Salonika front are interesting: here a multinational force held the Bulgarians at bay in mountainous northern Greece. Often considered a 'forgotten army', it nonetheless presided over the first surrender of a major Central Power, in October 1918.

Christmas cards were also sent to the front; with soldiers separated from their loved ones, it was inevitable that the Army Postal Service would be deluged with incoming mail. This was especially the case in the first Christmas of the war in 1914; and famously the King and Queen were to add to this burden in providing a Christmas card to accompany the magnificent gift from Princess Mary, in the form of a brass box filled with tobacco or other goods. The card depicted the royal couple, with King George V in appropriate naval or army uniform, depending on the service of the recipient. Like the box itself, these cards were often treasured by the recipient, and brought home as a souvenir.

The Royal postcard, as sent to all servicemen and women in 1914. There were two cards; one depicting the king in naval uniform (top), the other in army uniform (bottom). The centre card depicts the contents of the gift from Princess Mary.

47

Now, Woman has been called upon
And put upon her honour,
The boys can rest assured of this—
They can rely upon her.

THE HOME FRONT

A T HOME there was much to contend with, the pressures of fighting an increasingly widespread war starting to tell. Attacks on the British homeland had taken place in 1914 with naval bombardments – these caused outrage, and a flurry of postcards that depicted the aftermath of the attacks on the East Coast. As if this wasn't enough, air raids from airships commenced in 1914, bombers following in 1917–18. These caused widespread fear in major cities, and was to influence thinking in the post-war world. Unrestricted submarine warfare was declared by the Germans in February 1915, intended to starve the British, dependent as they were on imported goods. Almost thirteen million gross tons of shipping would be lost, the convoy system and the secret 'Q' Ships introduced as a response; the USA and Brazil would enter the war as a consequence. Food shortages were to become commonplace before rationing of certain goods was introduced in 1918.

GOING HOME

For the average soldier on the Western Front, leave would come only rarely – once a year if he was lucky, with officers having leave more frequently. Leave could be a frustrating experience for those based at the remote corners of the British Isles, as the journey would be long and arduous, and it was common for the soldier to return home in full kit, with the mud of Flanders still on his uniform. Not every soldier found it an easy experience; others would use the opportunity to wed their sweethearts – a popular photographic subject for postcards.

If official leave was a rarity, then getting a 'Blighty wound' – not too serious to be life threatening, not too slight to keep him overseas – was dreamed of as a means of escaping the front by most soldiers. Like many others before it, this idea passed across into popular culture, and postcards picked up the theme. War hospitals up and down the country were to receive soldiers 'from the front'. These were set up in large private houses and municipal buildings in order to satisfy the demand for suitable accommodation, and were often staffed by 'VADs', volunteer nurses belonging to the Voluntary Aid

Opposite:
The introduction of rationing in 1918, and food economy in general, was often used to illustrate postcards, as in this Raphael Tuck 'Oilette' card.

49

Right: Leave was a relatively rare occurrence; this card, drawn by D. Tempest and published by Bamforth, picks up on the emotion attached to the event of a return home.

Far right: A 'Blighty wound' – serious enough (but not life threatening) to get the soldier home – was hoped for by many soldiers. This card by Dudley Buxton captures the spirit of the event.

I was fairly taken off my feet when he came home!

LUCKY DEVIL!

Hand-illustrated hospital-issue postcard, sent from a wounded soldier. Such pieces are rare survivors.

Detachments, run by the British Red Cross Society and the Order of St John of Jerusalem. VAD nurses would serve alongside military nurses and Royal Army Medical Corps (RAMC) personnel in all war hospitals. War hospitals were set up the length and breadth of the country, to receive the mass of wounded soldiers that had made their way through the many stages – from Aid Post, Casualty Clearing Station, Base Hospital and Hospital Ship, amongst others – to home. Wounded and maimed soldiers would be a familiar sight, and the hospital trains arriving from the Channel ports would be met by anxious civilians.

Soldiers sent to hospital, and convalescent, were ordered out of their familiar khaki and into hospital blue, a simple suit of blue clothes worn with a distinctive red tie, and khaki Service Dress Cap, or other headdress appropriate to the regiment or nationality of the soldier. In general 'hospital blues' would provide a poor fit. Depicted in contemporary portraits are contrasting images of British soldiers in hospital blues: stoic British Tommies and an amputee, recently decorated with the Military Medal for bravery.

The blue uniform provided a distinctive sign of a wounded soldier's status, a badge of honour that distinguished him as a man from the front. Many postcards were produced, mirroring the general feeling of goodwill to wounded heroes in 'hospital blues' that was to persist throughout the war; crowds often

Wounded soldiers in 'hospital blues'.

Old Bills made like New!

"Little Boy Blue"
LITTLE BOY BLUE

At WEST KIRBY.

Come here, if you are in blues.

PRIVATE COPPIT: "I'M FEELING MUCH BETTER TO-DAY, NURSE!"
NURSE: "YES, AND YOU'RE LOOKING MUCH BETTER, TOO!"

'Hospital blues' were popular subjects for postcard publishers. The card top left was designed by soldier artist Bruce Bairnsfather for the Surrey Red Cross.

gathered to greet the wounded at the main railway termini. Convalescent soldiers would be a familiar sight, and in some rare cases, a tourist attraction.

The 'Loos Trenches' were one such tourist attraction, set up in the dunes of Lytham St Annes near Blackpool. With front-line and communication trenches, fire bays and traverses, and many other aspects of current military architecture, these trenches were intended to provide some sense of trench life for the visitor – rather like the preserved 'trench experiences' do today. With wounded soldiers in hospital blues as guides, these men undoubtedly had more to tell than could easily be shared with the casual day-trippers. The rear of the cards illustrated, sent by parent and child of the same family, reads: 'We have just been to the Loos trenches, it is a very instructive sight and there are hundreds of wounded soldiers to show visitors around'. Bizarre today, these postcards depict the result of a 'diverting time at the seaside' – completely detached from the reality of the front line.

'Loos Trenches', a tourist attraction near Blackpool manned by convalescent soldiers, and named after the battle of Loos in 1915. The 'Arras trenches' were a later incarnation from 1917.

BOMBARDMENTS AND AIR RAIDS

The war came close to home in December 1914, when the German navy carried out attacks against the British east coast towns of Scarborough, Hartlepool and Whitby. Shelling these towns from offshore, the Imperial German navy severely damaged streets in these towns, killing 137, and wounding a further 590. Postcards depicting this act – seen widely at the time as an atrocity against innocent civilians – were widely circulated. Further bombardments took place in 1916, at Yarmouth and Lowestoft, with a similar postcard response.

The first air attacks on Britain came from cumbersome Zeppelin airships, which bombed the east coast in January 1915, Great Yarmouth being the first town to be hit. Raids on London followed at the end of May, and were widely condemned as further evidence of German 'frightfulness', the raiders being described as 'baby killers'. However, the German airships were extremely vulnerable, and with the destruction of the wooden-framed Schütte-Lanz SLII by Lieutenant Leefe Robinson over Cuffley, Hertfordshire on 2–3 September 1916, the first over British soil, their days were numbered.

Robinson would be awarded the Victoria Cross, and be rightly celebrated in postcards. Sadly, he was to be shot down over France by Albatross fighters of Von Ricthtofen's *Jasta II* and later died of Spanish influenza in December 1918, following his release from Holzminden POW Camp.

The Zeppelin raids came largely to a halt in 1917, with almost three-quarters of the fleet of 115 airships destroyed or disabled. Postcards illustrating the destruction of the airships were well received; but the emphasis was soon to shift to Gotha bombers in the same year. Postcards celebrating the success of British airmen and static air defences against these 'baby killers' were extremely popular. In total, there were

The German bombardment of the north-east coast of England in 1914 was widely condemned, and was the subject of a range of photographic postcards illustrating the damage.

Postcards of the destruction of the Zeppelin 'baby-killers' were popular, and produced by a range of publishers, including a special, un-numbered, *Daily Mail* War Picture (*top left*).

fifty-one Zeppelin raids and fifty-two bomber raids on the United Kingdom, which together dropped 280 tons of bombs. The casualties amounted to 1,413 killed, and 3,409 wounded.

RATIONING

Rationing was first introduced in February 1918. Although there had been some concerns over panic buying and stockpiling in 1914, shortages were not felt until late 1916, after the introduction of unrestricted submarine warfare, a tactic employed by the Germans early in 1915. Much of Britain's food (around 60 per cent), was imported from Canada and the United States, and the action of the U-boats in sinking merchant ships crossing the Atlantic was a cause of great concern – particularly so when wheat started to run dangerously low in April 1916 following failure of the harvest. Food prices began to rise, and steps were taken to persuade people to voluntarily reduce their intake of bread, with the Royal Family taking the lead in promoting this trend. But as bread was a staple food, queues started to mount at high street shops, and not just for the humble loaf – meat, fats and sugar were also hard to obtain. In response, and following a variety of voluntary schemes,

The popular war savings 'Tank Banks' featured on many cards as they toured Britain.

compulsory rationing was finally introduced on the last day of 1917, with sugar the first commodity to be rationed. Meat and fats followed in April 1918 (although introduced earlier in the Home Counties). Typical weekly rations included fifteen ounces of meat, five ounces of bacon, four ounces of fats and eight ounces of sugar. Food queues gradually subsided, and ration books became commonplace and familiar. Not surprisingly, rationing (and, less obviously, food shortage) became a popular subject for postcards. Particular subjects include the use of potatoes as a good all-round food, and the persuasion of the public to be frugal with bread, the Government wishing to avoid the bread queues seen in other countries. In this way, postcards did their bit in this propaganda battleground.

WAR SAVINGS

Prosecuting a world war was costly, and the need for sufficient funds in the coffers led the Government to appeal for war savings from the public. Purchase of National War Bonds and War Savings Certificates was portrayed as a patriotic duty, allowing the money to be used in the development and construction of the materiel of war.

'Arf a 'mo', Kaiser!' Two of Bert Thomas's postcards raising funds for tobacco for the troops, through the *Weekly Despatch* newspaper.

Many novel approaches were in promoting war savings, none more so than the 'Tank Banks', which toured Britain in 1917. Following the debut of two Mark IV tanks at the Lord Mayor's Show in London during November 1917, the Government mobilised examples of these new 'wonder machines' to raise money and support from the sale of War Bonds and War Savings Certificates. Six Mark IV male tanks – *Egbert* (No 141), *Nelson* (No 130), *Julian* (No 113), *Old Bill* (No 119), *Drake* (No 137) and *Iron Rations* (No 142) were to tour Britain in 1918, raising millions of pounds through 'Tank Bank Weeks'. Each tank became the focal point for donation. Postcards of the tanks, particularly *Nelson*, were issued (together with tank moneyboxes and a range of ephemera produced in commemoration), usually with a range of captions, often 'Our Tank Bank', or 'One of Our Tanks'. These were popular wherever the tank made its appearance – and in fact tanks in general became a hit with the public. Many novelty tank postcards were produced, particularly by the specialist publisher E. T. W. Dennis & Sons, of Scarborough.

With the war's end, those boroughs that had raised the most money received a full-sized tank, usually displayed in parks and squares – the last survivor now stands in Ashford, Kent.

There were many calls on the public purse, particularly the provision of 'comforts' for the troops at the front. Cigarettes and tobacco were especially prized; smoking was a means of killing time, of filling the void between meals and routine. It was also a means of combating both the stench of the war, and in the Middle East at least, of deterring the plagues of flies. Famously, the *Weekly Despatch* newspaper organised a tobacco fund for the troops: 'Arf a 'mo' Kaiser!' Bert Thomas's famous drawing (reputedly sketched in minutes), together with less well-known versions, was reproduced on postcards as a means of drumming up support for this fund. It soon grew outside the confines of the scheme to personify the attitude of the British Tommy. Other comforts included funds for the construction of wooden huts in the rest areas close to the front; huts where men could relax after their tour of duty in the trenches. Perhaps intended to force the issue, photographic cards showing men at the front would be issued on behalf of the Australian Comforts Fund and the YMCA Hut Fund.

With the formation of the Ministry of Information in 1918, came official series of propaganda cards, initially promoting war savings. A set of cards was issued in 1918 by A. M. Davis & Co. of Finsbury Square, London to promote War Bonds. Reputedly drawn by noted military artist Harry Payne, this series of cards illustrates a range of heavy weapons, as well as rightly celebrating the work of the 'munitionettes'. These women would contribute greatly to the war effort, and were part of the groundswell in public opinion ensuring that women gained the vote in post-war Britain. They would be nicknamed 'canaries' due to their sallow skin caused by TNT poisoning; over a hundred women lost their lives to this invidious hazard. The 'War Bonds Campaign Post Cards' were issued in connection with the National War Savings Committee, the

YMCA hut fund charity postcards. The money raised went towards the construction of recreation huts at home and closer to the front.

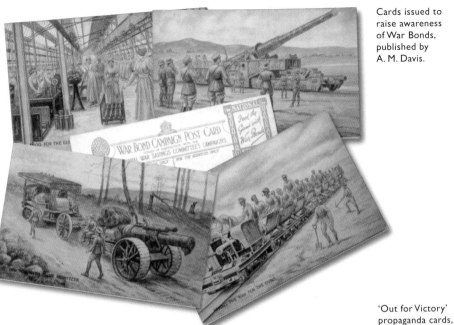

Cards issued to raise awareness of War Bonds, published by A. M. Davis.

illustrative material supplied by the newly formed Ministry of Information (MoI). They would all carry the slogan 'Feed the Guns with War Bonds'.

Also produced by the MoI in 1918 were the 'Out for Victory' series of cards, drawn by famous *Punch* artist Leonard Raven-Hill. The series illustrated a range of spirited individuals, each with a motto. Typical examples include 'Tommy' ('I want peace right enough – but I'll finish my job first') and 'The Allotment Holder' ('Too old to fight, but doing his bit to beat the U-boats'). No doubt produced when times were tough – the U-boat war biting deeply into British imports, and the army in France with their 'backs to the wall' – they must surely be evidence of the work of the Ministry of Information.

'Out for Victory' propaganda cards, illustrated by Leonard Raven-Hill; no publisher is indicated on the reverse.

L'YSER
1914-1918
2ᵉ Série

LOUVAIN
LES RUINES   THE RUINS

A Louvain, le 25 août 1914 et jours sui...   On the 25th of August 1914 and the fo...

RUINES
RUINS   D'YPRES   Halles et Cathédrale
Halls and Cathedral
Nᵒ 3

12 CARTES POSTALES
POSTCARDS

Hell Fire Co

MENIN GATE MEMORIAL YPRES
66.000 names
To the Armies of the British Empire who stood here from 1914 to 1918
and to those of their Dead who have no known grave.

AVANT
PENDANT et APRÈS
LA GUERRE   YPRES   Série Nᵒ 4

BEFORE
DURING and AFTER
THE WAR

RUINES de
RUINS of   D'YPRES   EN 1919
AND 1919   Nᵒ 4

12 CARTES POSTALES
POSTCARDS

ARRAS
AVANT ET APRÈS
LE

Ypres
Série 2.
British Front during the War 1914~1918

AVANT
PENDANT et APRÈS
LA GUERRE   YPRES   Série Nᵒ 3

BEFORE
DURING and AFTER
THE WAR

10 CARTES POSTALES
POSTCARDS   PHOTO ANTONY d'YPRES
DÉPOSÉ

REMEMBRANCE

FOR MANY, the end of the war came abruptly. The Central Powers had been crumbling during the autumn of 1918. Bulgaria was first to capitulate, on 29 September; the Ottoman Empire followed on 30 October, Austria-Hungary on 3 November, and finally Germany herself on 11 November. The terms of the armistice with Germany required the cessation of hostilities at 11 a.m. on 11 November, the evacuation of occupied territory, the surrender of large quantities of arms and equipment, and the disarming and internment of the High Seas Fleet. German soil was to be occupied west of the Rhine. For those troops not instructed to take on occupation duties, demobilisation could not come soon enough. Yet it would take many months to return Britain's citizen army back to its peacetime occupations.

Souvenirs of the Great War; photographic postcards of soldiers figure prominently.

The end of the war officially ended with the Armistice of 11 November 1918, after a succession of hammer blows that had fallen on the German Army since the opening of the Battle of Amiens on 8 August 1918 – the beginning of one hundred days of continuous advance. During this advance, the Allied armies pushed the Germans back to a line that was broadly similar to the one where it had first met the British 'Old Contemptibles', four years before. With the Armistice agreed, the war on the Western Front was to end abruptly, and the British Fourth and Second armies commenced their advance into Germany as an occupying power on 17 November. The news of the end of the war was received in many ways – for the soldiers, its occurrence was almost a matter of fact. Winning the peace would be a major challenge.

Opposite: Postcards of the ruins and wartime destruction were sold in booklets and single cards to post-war battlefield tourists.

IN MEMORIAM

As men were killed, so long lists of casualties were published in local newspapers, and 'Rolls of Honour' issued. For those able to do so, a common way of extending the mourning process and alerting local communities to the loss of a loved one was to have 'In Memoriam' cards printed, in varying styles; some as postcards, others as black-edged folding cards. Often, these incorporated a regimental badge or other military device, and usually an image of the soldier himself. Many thousands must have been printed as the war took its course.

For those bereaved, knowing that a loved one had been decently buried by his comrades-in-arms was some comfort. The Imperial War Graves Commission (IWGC) was set up during the war, in 1917, in order to care for the graves of the fallen. It was decided early on that there should be no repatriation, the men and women being buried as close as possible to the site of death. With graves scattered across the world, visiting them was a daunting proposition. This was particularly so for far-flung corners in the Middle East and Africa, and the IWGC would supply postcard photographs of these gravesites to relatives on request. That of Second Aircraftsman Henry Lucas of the Royal Flying Corps, who died in 1917 and is buried at Hadra Cemetery, Alexandria in Egypt is typical.

France and Flanders was nearer, and a post-war industry was developed to cater for the numbers of people who travelled to visit their loved ones, and to visit the sites of battle. Among them, cards depicting war damage were popular; during

Above: 'In memoriam' postcards privately printed by bereaved families. Private Johnson is buried at Hill 10 Cemetery, in Suvla Bay.

Right: Imperial War Graves Commission (now Commonwealth War Graves Commission) photographic card of a war grave. such cards were sent on request to families. Second Aircraftsman Henry Lucas, of the Royal Flying Corps, is buried at Hadra Cemetery, in Egypt.

the war the same cards were used to underline the 'frightfulness' of the German military machine, intent on the destruction of some of Europe's finest architectural jewels. After the war, most were produced in booklet form as souvenirs; the cards could be torn out for use. Famous are the cards produced in a variety of formats by photographers Anthony of Ypres; these catalogue the steady descent of Ypres from a proud Medieval city to a ruin so complete that it would take decades to rebuild. For most people, with no chance of pilgrimage to the grave of a son or husband, local war memorials would attain the greatest significance; none more so than the Cenotaph.

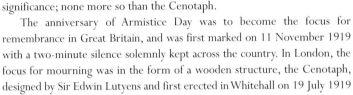

Cities in flames; these French cards were popular souvenirs of war.

The anniversary of Armistice Day was to become the focus for remembrance in Great Britain, and was first marked on 11 November 1919 with a two-minute silence solemnly kept across the country. In London, the focus for mourning was in the form of a wooden structure, the Cenotaph, designed by Sir Edwin Lutyens and first erected in Whitehall on 19 July 1919 as part of the Victory celebrations – its sombre form representing the fallen soldiers. Spontaneously, this wooden structure was to become a focal point for mourning. It was to be replaced by a permanent version in Portland Stone, completed in time for 11 November 1920. The structure has remained the focal point for the nation's remembrance service ever since, and has been a popular subject on postcards. The Unknown Soldier, a soldier plucked from an unidentified grave in France and representative of the many fallen sons, was also to be buried in Westminster Abbey as part of this commemoration, his grave appearing on many cards.

The Cenotaph, Whitehall.

The Cenotaph was a popular postcard subject.

A LAND FIT FOR HEROES'

It is a cliché that soldiers returned from the war expecting a 'land fit for heroes'. In fact, with so many men demobilised, and in the depth of a post-war slump following the gearing of a nation for 'total war', finding employment was a nightmare task. For those disabled, there were few choices, although for those blinded, St Dunstan's provided a lifeline. Arthur Pearson, proprietor of the *Evening Standard*, set up St Dunstan's in 1915. Pearson was himself blind, and believed that given training, servicemen who had lost their sight during the war could have their lives transformed, to lead independent lives. His organisation, based firstly in Regents Park in London, helped give hope to those who had been disabled; it was funded by charity, through donations, or the sale of cards illustrated. Other ex-soldiers, like George Eames, 'the soldier baritone', blinded on the Somme, would find their own way. For many others, charity, and the sale of small goods like matches, or cards like those illustrated would be the only way of scratching a living in the 'land fit for heroes'.

Charity postcards in high Edwardian style by Boer War artist R. Caton-Woodville, here raising money for St Dunstan's.

'Land fit for heroes': postcards like these were printed and sold to raise money for unemployed ex-servicemen.

FURTHER READING

Alderson, F. *The Comic Postcard in English Life*. David & Charles, Newton Abbot, 1970.

Bryant, M. *World War 1 in Cartoons*. Grub Street, London, 2006.

Byatt, A. *Picture Postcards and their Publishers*. Golden Age, Malvern, 1978.

Currie, B. *The First World War in Old Picture Postcards*. European Library, Zaltbommel, 1988.

Doyle, P. *Tommy's War. British Military Memorabilia 1914–1918*. Crowood, Marlborough, 2008.

Doyle, P. *The British Soldier of the First World War*. Shire, Oxford, 2008.

Hill, C.W. *Picture Postcards*. Shire, Princes Risborough, 1999.

Holt, T. and V. *Picture Postcards of the Golden Age: A Collector's Guide*. MacGibbon & Kee, London, 1971.

Holt, T. and V. *Till the Boys Come Home. The Picture Postcards of the First World War*. Macdonald & Jane's, London, 1977.

Kennedy, A. and Crabb, G. *The Postal History of the British Army in World War 1*. George Crabb, Epsom, 1977.

Laffin, J. *World War 1 in Postcards*. Alan Sutton, Gloucester, 1988.

McDonald, I. *The Boer War in Postcards*. Wrens Park, London, 1990.

Messenger, C. *Call to Arms. The British Army 1914–1918*. Weidenfield & Nicholson, London, 2005.

Monahan, V. *Collecting Postcards in Colour, 1914–1930*. Blandford Press, Poole, 1980.

Rikards, M. and Moody, M. *The First World War, Ephemera, Mementoes, Documents*. Jupiter Books, London, 1975.

Roberts, A. *Postcards from the Trenches. Images of the First World War*. Bodleian Library, Oxford, 2008.

INDEX